Travellers' Tales

I Talk You Talk Press

CONTENTS

1. DON'T GO WITHOUT ME!

Fernanda was on a bus going from London to Scotland. She was a student from Brazil. It was the winter break, so she had some free time. She decided to visit Scotland. She didn't have much money, so she was taking the bus instead of the train.

She looked at her watch. It was 11:00pm. She looked around the bus. Most of the other passengers were asleep. She wanted to sleep, but it was uncomfortable. She looked out of the window. It was dark, so she couldn't see much.

I hope we stop for a break soon, she thought. *I want to stretch.*

Thirty minutes later, the driver said, "We're going to stop for a short break at the next service station. We'll stop for twenty minutes. The service station is open. It sells food, and there are toilets. Please don't be late coming back to the bus."

Good! We are stopping! thought Fernanda.

The bus drove into the service station. Fernanda and some of the other passengers got off the bus. It was cold outside. There were no cars in the car park. The service station was very small.

Fernanda went to the café. *I'm hungry,* she thought. *I'll buy a hot sandwich.*

She walked up to the counter. "Can I have a hot cheese and ham sandwich, please?" she asked the man.

"Yes. But it will take ten minutes," said the man.

"That's OK," said Fernanda. She paid for the sandwich and sat down at a table.

Ten minutes later, the man brought her the sandwich.

Should I eat it now, or should I eat it on the bus? she thought. She looked at her watch. *I'll eat it now. The bus will leave in another ten minutes.*

The sandwich was very hot, but it was good. When Fernanda finished eating, she looked at her watch. *I have five minutes. I'll go to the toilet.*

Fernanda walked to the toilets. When she finished using the toilet, she walked outside. She looked around the car park. She couldn't see the bus.

"Where's the bus?" she asked herself. She looked to the left. She could see the bus driving away.

She started to run after the bus. "Wait! Don't go without me!" she shouted. But it was too late. The bus drove back onto the motorway and disappeared.

No! What am I going to do? My suitcase is on that bus! I'm in the middle of the countryside, and it's almost midnight!

Fernanda wanted to cry. *OK, I have to be strong,* she thought. *I'll call the bus company.*

She took out her phone. *Oh no! I have no signal! I can't make any calls! What can I do?*

She looked at the service station. *I can ask the man in the café to help me.*

She walked back into the café. The man was standing behind the counter. He looked bored.

"Excuse me," said Fernanda. "I need your help. I came on the bus from London. I went to the toilet, and the bus left without me. I have no signal on my phone, so I can't call the bus company. My suitcase is on the bus, and…"

Fernanda started to cry.

"That's terrible," said the man. He was a young man. He was about 25 years old. He smiled. "Don't worry. I can try to call the bus company." He went into a back room. A few minutes later, he came back.

"I'm sorry. There's no answer. The bus company office is closed."

"What am I going to do?" asked Fernanda. "I have nowhere to go!"

"This café closes in ten minutes. You can't stay here," said the man.

"I can't sleep outside! It's too cold! I'll die!" said Fernanda.

The man looked at her. Then he went into the back room.

Fernanda sat at a table and cried.

A few minutes later, the man came back. "I live with my girlfriend," he said. "I just called her and told her about you. She said you can come and stay with us tonight."

Fernanda looked at the man. "Really? Oh, that's so kind of you!" she said. She felt better.

"I'm Ian," said the man. "What's your name?"

"Fernanda. I'm a student from Brazil. I'm studying English in London."

"Nice to meet you," said Ian. "I'll finish work in thirty minutes. Here's a cup of tea for you to drink while you wait."

He gave Fernanda the cup of tea.

"Thank you so much," said Fernanda. She sat at a table and waited for the man to finish work.

Forty minutes later, Fernanda and Ian were in his car.

"Where are we?" asked Fernanda.

"We are not far from Nottingham," said Ian.

"Where's that?" asked Fernanda.

"The middle of England," said Ian.

Ian drove on the motorway for about fifteen minutes, then he drove off the motorway.

"I live in a small town near here," he said. "We'll be at my flat in about ten minutes."

"This is so kind of you and your girlfriend," said Fernanda. "Thank you very much."

"Don't mention it," said the man. "I couldn't leave you at the service station. You're a young woman travelling alone."

A few minutes later, Ian drove into a car park. "Here we are," he said. He stopped the car, and they got out.

They walked to Ian's flat. He lived on the third floor. They walked up the stairs. Ian opened the door. A woman was waiting in the flat.

"Hi! I'm Angela," she said. "Ian told me about you. It's terrible! Are you OK?"

Fernanda smiled. "Yes, I'm OK. I'm Fernanda. Thank you so much for letting me stay."

"That's OK. Are you hungry?" asked Angela.

"No, but I'm very tired," said Fernanda.

"We only have one bedroom, so you'll have to sleep on the sofa. Is that OK?" asked Angela.

"Yes, that's fine. Thank you so much," said Fernanda.

"In the morning, I'll call the bus company and complain," said Ian.

"How will I get to Scotland? The bus company has my suitcase. My suitcase will be in Scotland, and I'll be in the middle of England," said Fernanda.

"Don't worry about that," said Angela. "We will talk to the bus company tomorrow. Try to sleep tonight."

Angela gave Fernanda some blankets. Fernanda took her shoes off and lay down on the sofa. Angela switched the light off. Fernanda soon fell asleep.

When she woke up the next morning, she could smell coffee and toast.

"I made some breakfast for you," said Angela. "Did you sleep well?"

"Yes, thank you," said Fernanda. Angela brought her a cup of coffee and some eggs on toast.

"Thank you so much," said Fernanda. "I'm hungry." She ate and drank.

Ian came into the living room.

"I checked on the Internet. The bus company office is open. So I'm going to call them now," he said.

Fernanda listened to Ian talking to the bus company. She couldn't understand everything, but Ian sounded angry. A few minutes later, Ian hung up. He smiled at Fernanda.

"Everything is OK. The next bus to Scotland will stop at the service station in two hours. There is some space on the bus. You can ride on that bus. The bus company will keep your suitcase safe. It will be waiting for you when you arrive in Scotland. The woman in the office said she was very sorry to hear your story. The company will give you your money back. They will also pay for your return journey to London."

"Oh, that's great! Thank you so much!" said Fernanda.

For the next hour, Fernanda talked to Angela and Ian. They talked about Brazil, and England.

Ian looked at his watch. "I'll take you to the service station. I don't want you to miss the bus," he said.

"Thank you so much," said Fernanda. "You saved me!"

Ian and Angela smiled. "You're welcome," said Angela. "Ian and I like to travel very much. I hope we can go to Brazil one day. If we go to Brazil, please help us!"

"Of course!" said Fernanda. "My study in England will finish in six months. Then I'm going back to Brazil. I'm from Rio de Janeiro. Why don't you come and visit?"

Ian and Angela looked at each other. "That's a great idea!" said Ian.

"Yes, let's do it!" said Angela.

"You can stay at my house. So you only need to pay for flights," said Fernanda.

"We can save up some money this year, and go next year," said Angela. "Thank you!"

They became Facebook friends, and followed each other on Instagram.

"We can keep in touch online," said Angela. She looked at the time.
"You should go now," she said. "You don't want to miss the bus! See you in Brazil!"

2. LONELY IN KYOTO

Justin was from Australia. He was backpacking around Japan for two months. He had lost his job in Australia. He decided to travel before looking for a new job. It was spring, and the cherry blossoms were in bloom. He was in Kyoto. It was very beautiful. He enjoyed visiting the temples. There were many tourists, but Justin was lonely. He was a very shy man, and found it difficult to make new friends. He had spoken to people in restaurants, hotels and shops, but he hadn't spoken to anyone else.

One Saturday night, he was walking down a street. There were many restaurants in the street, and many people. The people were laughing and talking.

I want to eat dinner with someone tonight, he thought. *I don't want to eat alone again. But I can't ask strangers to eat with me. I'm so lonely. I don't want to travel alone again. Next time, I'll ask a friend to come travelling with me.*

Justin looked in the restaurant windows. Everyone was in groups. No one was eating alone. He didn't want to go into a restaurant alone again.

I'll buy some food and beer in a convenience store, and eat and drink in my hotel room, he thought. *It's not the best way to spend a Saturday night, but I can go on Facebook and chat with my friends back home.*

Justin saw a convenience store and walked towards it. Suddenly, he heard someone calling his name.

"Justin? Justin!" said a voice.

Justin looked around. A man was standing near him. He was looking at him. Justin looked at the man carefully.

"Pedro?" he said. "Is that you?"

"Yes!" said the man. "It's me! I don't believe it!"

The two men started to laugh. "I don't believe it either!" said Justin. "I haven't seen you since we left high school ten years ago! What are the chances of us meeting on a street in Kyoto?"

"I know! This is unbelievable! What are you doing here? Are you working?" asked Pedro.

"No, I'm backpacking around Japan. How about you?" asked Justin.

"I'm teaching English here. I've been here for two years," said Pedro.

"That's great!" said Justin.

"Where are you going?" asked Pedro.

"To a convenience store. I'm going to buy some food and beer to take back to my hotel room," said Justin.

"What? You can't do that! It's Saturday night! You can't spend it alone!" said Pedro.

"I have no friends here, and it's difficult for me to make friends," said Justin.

Pedro nodded. "I remember you from school. You were very shy. I'm going to a party. Come with me. You can meet some of my co-workers and students."

"That sounds great!" said Justin.

The two men walked to a restaurant. "The party is here," said Pedro.

They went inside. The waitress took them to a large room. There were many people there. They were eating and drinking.

"Hey, Pedro!" shouted a man. "You're here at last!"

"Listen everyone! Something unbelievable happened!" said Pedro. Everyone became quiet.

"I was walking down the street, and I saw this man. This is Justin. He is an old friend from high school. I haven't seen him for more than ten years! And then suddenly, I saw him on a street here in Kyoto!" said Pedro.

"Wow! That's amazing!" said a Japanese woman.

"If you are Pedro's friend, then you are our friend," said a man. "Come and join us. We have beer and lots of food!"

Justin smiled. "Thank you!"

He sat down at the table.

"Are you travelling around Japan?" asked a Japanese man.

"Yes, I am. I've been to Tokyo, Tohoku, Kanazawa and now Kyoto," said Justin.

"Wow! You've been to many places," said the man.

"Which is your favourite place?" asked a Japanese woman.

"I like Kyoto," said Justin. "It's very beautiful. I love the temples."

"I'm happy to hear that!" said the woman.

The man poured beer into Justin's glass. "Come on, drink!" he said.

Justin smiled and drank. He also ate some sashimi and tempura. The food was good. Pedro came over to him.

"Are you having a good time?" he asked.

"Yes, this is better than eating convenience store food in my hotel!" said Justin.

Many other people came over to Justin to talk. He didn't feel shy anymore, and he started to relax. An older Japanese man came over to him.

"Do you like Japan?" he asked.

"Yes, I do. I like it very much," said Justin.

"What's your job in Australia?" asked the man.

"I don't have a job," said Justin. "I lost my job a few months ago. I used to work in a book shop."

"Would you like to work in Japan?" asked the man.

"Work in Japan? I've never thought about it," said Justin.

"I'm the owner of a language school here. If you want a job, you can come and work for me. Pedro works for me. And the Japanese people here are our students."

The man gave Justin his business card.

"Think about it," said the man. "And then email me."

Justin drank some beer. Then he smiled at the man. "I've thought about it," he said. "And the answer is yes! I'd love to work here in Kyoto!"

"Great!" said the man. "When you get back to Australia, email me, and then I'll start the paperwork. I think the students will like you."

The man went away. Justin smiled. *This night is amazing,* he thought. *I had no friends here. I was going to eat dinner in my hotel room. Then I saw an old school friend and now I have a new job! We never know what can happen when we travel!*

3. I'M ALWAYS RIGHT!

Amir and Lena were excited. They were in Switzerland for a snowboarding holiday. They had never been snowboarding before. They were going to stay for a week.

They had arrived at their chalet the day before. The chalet was big. It had a large living room, a big bedroom and a kitchen. From the windows, they could see the ski and snowboard slopes.

"This is going to be the best holiday ever!" said Amir. "But it was expensive. The insurance you bought was expensive, too."

"We need the insurance," said Lena. "We have never been snowboarding before. We might have an accident. If we have an accident, it will cost a lot of money."

Amir laughed. "We won't have an accident! Snowboarding is easy! I watched the Winter Olympics on TV. I can do that."

Lena looked at Amir. She was worried. "It's more difficult than it looks," said Lena.

"You worry too much!" said Amir. He looked at the clock. "It's ten am. Let's go to the slopes!"

Thirty minutes later, Amir and Lena were at the bottom of a slope. An instructor was with them.

"It's our first time, so we need lessons," said Lena.

"Sure, I'll teach you the basics," said the instructor. "My name is Francois. We will use the beginner slope."

Amir laughed. "The beginner slope? That's too easy. I want to use the big slope, over there."

"That's for experienced snowboarders," said Francois. "I can't let you go on there. It's too dangerous."

Amir sighed. "OK, but I don't need lessons. I'm going to teach myself."

Lena looked at her husband. "Amir," she said. "We need lessons."

"You need lessons, but I don't," said Amir. "I'm not having lessons."

Francois and Lena looked at Amir.

"OK," said Francois. "But you must stay on the beginner slope."

"OK, OK," said Amir.

They got their snowboards and walked to the lift to the beginner slope. They took the lift. It wasn't so far. The beginner slope was not very high. They got off and stood on their snowboards.

"OK, let's start here," said Francois to Lena. "First…"

"Lena! Look at me! I can do it!" shouted Amir.

Lena and Francois watched Amir. He snowboarded down the slope for a few seconds, and then he shouted. "Help! I can't stop!" Then, he fell over. He landed very hard on the snow. Francois and Lena got off their snowboards and ran to Amir.

"Amir! Are you OK?" asked Lena.

"No! I can't move my right leg! I think it's broken!" said Amir.

Francois looked at him. "Where does it hurt?" he asked.

"Here," said Amir, pointing to his hip. "And here." He pointed to his knee.

"Can you move?" asked Francois.

"No, I can't move at all!" said Amir.

"I'll call for the emergency helicopter to come," said Francois.

"I'm so sorry for the trouble," said Lena. She looked at Amir. "Why didn't you wait and have lessons before you tried snowboarding?" she asked. She was angry.

"I'm sorry," said Amir.

A few minutes later, a helicopter came. Some men put Amir on a stretcher and put him in the helicopter. Lena and Francois also rode in the helicopter. They went to the local hospital.

In the hospital, the doctors looked at Amir's leg. Lena waited in the waiting room. After about thirty minutes, the doctors came out to Lena.

"I'm sorry to tell you this, but your husband has broken his hip and knee. He will need two operations," said one of the doctors. "Do you have insurance?"

"Yes, we do," said Lena.

"Good," said the doctor. "Because it's expensive."

"How long will my husband be in hospital?" asked Lena.

"About two months," said one of the doctors.

"Two months? But we are only here for a week! We have to go back to work next week, and...."

"Your husband won't be going back to work next week. He will be here for two months," said the doctor.

Lena was shocked. "Can I see him?" she asked.

"Yes, of course," said the doctor.

Lena walked into Amir's room. When she saw him, she didn't feel bad for him. She felt angry.

"Why didn't you listen to me? I told you we needed lessons! You watch the Olympics and you think you can snowboard like those athletes! You never listen to me!"

Amir looked sad. "I'm sorry Lena," he said.

"And you said we didn't need insurance! Aren't you glad I got insurance for you?" asked Lena.

"Yes, of course. I'm sorry," said Amir. "How long am I going to be in here for?"

"Two months! You need two operations!" said Lena.

"Two months? But what about work?" asked Amir.

"Well, you can't go! I'll call your boss tomorrow."

Amir reached out his hand. "I'm so sorry Lena. I should have listened to you. Are you going to stay with me for two months? Please stay with me."

Lena looked at Amir. "No, I'm not. I have to work from next week," she said.

"What? You are going to leave me here, alone? But I'm your husband!" said Amir.

"And I'm your wife! When I tell you something, listen to me! You will have a lot of time to think about that while you are here in hospital!" said Lena. "This will be a good lesson for you! In the future, listen to me! I'm always right!"

4. AN ISLAND EXPERIENCE

Wanda worked in a school in Los Angeles. She taught six- and seven-year-old children. She liked her job very much, but she missed her family. They lived in Denver.

Wanda's birthday was in May. She was 25 years old. When she came home from work, she looked in her mailbox. There were some letters and a card from her brother in Denver. She sat at the desk in her small apartment and read her mail.

The card from her brother, Alex, said

---Happy birthday Sis! I couldn't think what to buy you for a present. So I bought you a raffle ticket. Maybe you will be lucky and win!---

Wanda felt angry. *Alex is so lazy. A raffle ticket is not a real present!* She didn't read the ticket. She put it in a drawer of her desk and forgot about it.

Six weeks later, Wanda got a message on her smartphone.

---Dear Ms Fritton. We are pleased to tell you that you won first prize in our raffle. Please contact us, so you can make plans for your magic island holiday.---

Wanda could not believe it. *I won a raffle! I must be careful. Maybe it's not real. I must check. Where is the ticket? What is the prize?*

It took a long time. Finally, Wanda found the ticket in her desk drawer. The raffle was to make money for education of poor children in the South Pacific. The charity was called Bislama Plus. She looked for Bislama Plus on the Internet. She found all their contact details.

I want to be careful. I won't email them or text them. I'll use the telephone. It'll be safer.

Wanda called Bislama Plus. The woman she spoke to was very

nice. "Congratulations!" she said. "You'll have a wonderful holiday. Please go to Pacific Magic. They are a big travel agency. Where do you live?"

"In Los Angeles," said Wanda.

"Good! Pacific Magic has an office there. Take your passport and your driver's licence so they know who you are."

The holiday package was for two people.

Wanda asked her friend from the school to go with her. Her friend's name was Felice.

"It'll be wonderful," said Wanda. "We'll fly to New Caledonia. Then we'll take a helicopter to an island. On the island is a luxury hotel. We can have massages and beauty treatments. We can go sailing, swimming and underwater diving. Everything is free!"

Felice and Wanda were very excited. They planned to take the trip during school vacation.

The flight from Los Angeles to New Caledonia was very long, but they were able to sleep. When they arrived in New Caledonia, they went through immigration and picked up their bags.

There was a man standing in the airport holding a sign. It said

--- *Pacific Magic Luxury Vacations – Wanda Fritton*---

The two women hurried over to the man.

"I'm Wanda Fritton," said Wanda. "This is my friend Felice James. Are you our helicopter pilot?"

The man smiled. "Yes. I'm Earl. I'm your helicopter pilot. Everything is ready. We can leave now."

Earl took them to another part of the airport. The helicopter was waiting. Felice was nervous. "I've never been on a helicopter before."

"I've been flying helicopters for twenty years," said Earl. "You'll be safe with me."

They climbed onto the helicopter. "The flight will take about one hour and fifteen minutes," said Earl. "It will be a little noisy, so please wear these headphones. If I want to tell you something, I want to be sure you can hear me."

It was a wonderful experience. When Wanda and Felice looked down at the ocean, they could see blue-green sea and tiny coral islands. But suddenly, after about 30 minutes, there was a loud noise. Even with their headphones on, Wanda and Felice could hear it. It seemed to come from far away. The helicopter shook.

"What's that?" shouted Felice. She held Wanda's hand.

Wanda watched Earl. He was looking at his control panel and talking on the radio.

She looked out of the window. It had been a beautiful clear day, but now the sky was darker.

Then Earl spoke to them. "I don't want you to worry," he said. "A volcano has erupted. It is far from here, but the gas and dust from the volcano have entered the sky. Maybe it will be dangerous for us to continue to the resort island. I want you to be safe. I'm going to land the helicopter on a very small island near here."

Earl took the helicopter down very low. The sky was clear there. He was talking all the time on the radio and watching his control panel. They flew lower and lower. They could see the palm trees. They were next to the palm trees! Then the helicopter landed very gently on a beach.

"Stay here, please," said Earl. He climbed out of the helicopter and bent over as he ran towards the palm trees.

They could see people running towards Earl. The people were very excited. They were shouting and waving their arms.

Earl talked to the island people. When he came back, he said, "Everything is OK. There's a village behind the coconut palm trees. I've spoken to the headman. You can stay in the village. You must be very careful when you get out of the helicopter. Bend down and stay low while you are walking. I don't want you to get hit by the rotor blades. Don't worry about your bags. The village people will bring them to you. Do you speak French?"

"Uh, no," said Wanda.

"I know a little French," said Felice.

"The people here speak their own language. Some of them also speak Bislama and French. They will look after you. Get out now and go with them. I must tie the helicopter down, and then I'll stay with it. The people here have seen helicopters in the sky sometimes, but they have never seen one up close. They are very honest, but they will want to touch everything! I don't want any damage."

Wanda and Felice went with the happy smiling people to the village. The houses were very small, but in the middle of the village was a bigger building. It seemed to be a hall or meeting house.

Felice was listening hard. "I think we can sleep in that big building," she said. "They will bring us food and drink."

The two women sat on mats on the ground. Young boys came

with coconuts and showed them how to drink the coconut milk from the nuts. Then some women came with food. Everything was very strange and different. The people were shy, but they were kind. Felice was happy because she could understand them a little.

Wanda and Felice stayed in the village for two days. It was an interesting time. The food was very fresh and tasted good. They ate coconuts, fish, vegetables and eggs.

They learned that the meeting house was also the school and the medical centre. The children's schoolbooks all had a label on them. The label said 'Bislama Plus'.

"That's the charity, I won the raffle from," said Wanda.

One of the older women was the teacher, and another was a trained nurse. They spoke French, but Felice was often in trouble because their French was better than hers.

"They talk so quickly!" she said. "I have to ask them to slow down."

Finally on the second day, Earl came to the village. "I have been talking on my satellite phone. It's safe for us to leave now. You'll be at the luxury resort very soon. I'll go back to the helicopter. Please come as soon as you can."

Wanda and Felice tried to give the headman money, but he wouldn't take it. They searched their bags to find gifts. They found pens, combs, scarves, hats and T-shirts, but they had nothing to give the children.

Everyone from the village walked back with them to the helicopter. They were singing. They stopped at the coconut palm trees and the headman made a long speech. The schoolteacher translated from the island language into French. Then Wanda and Felice were given coconuts, fruit and fish.

"They are worried we won't have good food to eat," said Felice.

When they were on the helicopter, Wanda and Felice were crying.

"I feel bad," said Wanda. "We are going to a luxury resort. These people have so little, but they are kind. I don't want to change their lifestyle, but I want to make it easier."

"Me too. We will work for Bislama Plus," said Felice. "We'll learn Bislama and we'll come back."

The helicopter rose high in the air. The village people were waving. Wanda and Felice waved back.

5. THEY TRICKED US!

Laura and Greg were excited. They were going to Italy for their honeymoon. They had just graduated, and they planned to spend ten days in Italy, before they started their first jobs. They had saved the wages from their part-time jobs. So they had just enough money, if they were very careful.

The first day of their honeymoon was perfect. They arrived in Rome very early in the morning. They caught a bus from the airport to the train station and took a train to Florence. Laura had booked a room in a small hotel. In the evening, they ate in a trattoria near the hotel. They sat outside in the garden. They ate pizzas and drank wine.

"This is perfect," said Laura. "I'm so pleased we didn't have a short American honeymoon in Las Vegas or Niagara Falls."

Greg laughed. "No! This is much better. We are lucky that you can speak Italian. I can only speak English. If I arranged our trip, we could only go to big tourist hotels where everyone speaks English. That would be too expensive for us."

"Yes," said Laura. "My father's parents went from Italy to the USA many years ago. They always talk in Italian at home, so I learned a lot. My family was very pleased when I studied Italian at university. But this is my first visit to Italy."

"And we'll go to your grandparents' home village," said Greg. "It'll be a great experience."

The next day was not so good. Greg and Laura planned to take a bus to Pisa. They waited at the bus stop. They waited a long time. The bus didn't come.

"What can we do?" asked Greg.

"I will go and ask someone in the bus office," said Laura.

Laura walked away. A bus came and stopped. Greg didn't know what to do. *I can't read the signs. Is that our bus? Where is Laura?*

The bus drove away.

Laura ran up to Greg. "Our bus is coming now!"

Greg was unhappy. "No, Laura," he said. "Our bus came, and it has gone."

"Oh no!" shouted Laura. "The next bus is at six tonight!"

"It's OK," said Greg. "We'll wait."

Greg and Laura sat down on their backpacks.

After a long time, a van stopped next to the bus stop. There were two men in the front of the van. "Where are you going?" the driver shouted in English.

"To Pisa!" shouted Laura

"OK! No problem. We can take you there."

Laura and Greg jumped up. They took their backpacks and got into the van.

"Thank you!" said Greg.

Greg and Laura sat in the back of the van. "Italians are very kind," said Greg.

"Maybe," said Laura very quietly. "The man talked in English. Are they Italians?"

After a few minutes, Laura called out the driver in Italian. "Is this the way to Pisa? I thought there was a big motorway."

The driver didn't answer. So Laura asked again in English. "Why did you leave the motorway?"

"You are tourists," answered the driver. "The motorway is boring. We will drive along the small roads. It will be more interesting for you."

They travelled far into the countryside. Suddenly, the van stopped.

"Oh no!" shouted the driver. "We have engine trouble. Please get out and push the van."

Laura and Greg jumped out onto the road. "Please push," said the driver.

Greg and Laura ran to the back of the van.

The van started quickly. It drove away. Laura and Greg were standing on the road. The two men in the van were laughing.

"Oh no!" shouted Greg. "They tricked us!"

"They have our backpacks. They have our money." Laura wanted to cry. "What can we do?"

Greg hugged Laura. "It's not so bad. I have my phone, our air tickets and our passports in my pockets. It will be OK."

Laura did not believe him. They stood by the side of the road. Laura was crying.

Then a small truck stopped next to them. A very small old man got out.

"Are you OK?" he asked in Italian.

"No!" answered Laura. "Two men in a van gave us a ride. Then the van stopped, and the driver asked us to push. As soon as we got out, he drove away. They have all our money and our backpacks."

"I'll take you to the police station in the next town," said the old man. "You must tell the policeman about the bad men. Maybe the police can help you."

The old man took them to the police station. The policeman was very nice. Laura told him what had happened.

"This has happened before," said the policeman. "There are two men who look for tourists. I don't think they are Italians. They speak in English, so the tourists are happy. They offer to help the tourists. Then they find a way to steal from them. Did you see the licence number on the van?"

"No," said Laura. "I didn't think to look."

She told Greg what the policeman had said. "Did you see the licence number of the van?" she asked.

"No," said Greg. "The van was grey, but it was very dirty. The licence number was covered in mud."

Laura translated Greg's words for the policeman.

"We'll try to find the van," said the policeman. "Where will you stay? I'll call you when we have information."

Laura started crying again. "We have nowhere to stay. We have no money."

Suddenly the old man spoke. "They will stay with me and my family. You know me. I'm Franco Berti. Call my house when you have information."

"OK," said the policeman. "I hope I'll have some information soon."

Outside the police station, Laura thanked the old man.

"You are very kind," she said.

The old man said, "I am angry. These bad men are not from this place. We like tourists to come here. So I want to help you. My name is Franco Berti. I live in Cusignano. It's a very small village."

"What!" shouted Laura. She was very surprised. "We planned to go there. My grandparents came from that village."

Signore Berti looked at her. "What are their names?"

"Simone and Massimo Ricci. They went to the USA, many years ago."

"Yes," said Signore Berti. "I remember. My wife is Simone Ricci's cousin. She will be very pleased to meet you. Everyone in the village will want to meet you. Your grandparents never came back to Cusignano. Why didn't they come?"

"They made a good life in the USA. But there were many children. They didn't have enough money."

"I understand," said Signore Berti.

"Laura!" shouted Greg. "I don't understand anything. What's happening?"

"Oh Greg. I'm sorry. This is Signore Berti. He is very kind. When he heard we had no money and nowhere to stay, he invited us to his house. The police will try to find the men who stole our money and backpacks. If they have information, they will call him. But the amazing thing is that he lives in Cusignano! His wife is my grandmother's cousin!"

Greg could not believe it. "Wow! It's an unlucky day for us, but it's also a lucky day."

Laura and Greg stayed with Signore Berti and his wife Clara for a few days. Many people in the village remembered Laura's grandparents. Laura and Greg were invited to eat everywhere in the village. They used Greg's phone to take many photographs. Everyone wanted to hear about life in the USA. Some of the younger people in the village spoke English so Greg was happy. They had a wonderful time.

But they were also worried because they had no money. "How will we get to Rome?" Greg asked Laura. "If we miss our flight, we will lose our air ticket fares. And we will be late to start our new jobs. We must call our parents and ask them to send us some money."

"I agree," said Laura. "But I asked Signore Berti. He says it will take maybe a week or ten days before the money arrives. The money will come too late. It's OK. He has a plan."

Signore Berti's plan was very good.

"I will drive you to Florence," he said. "My brother's son lives in Florence. He drives a bus. He will take a junior soccer team to Rome to play a game. He will leave the day before your flight. There is room on the bus for you.

"And I will lend you some money. Enough for a night in a small hotel in Rome, for a bus to the airport and for some food. When you are back in the USA, and you start your new jobs, you can send me the money."

The morning before they left, Signore Berti got a call from the police. He talked for a long time.

Then he talked to Laura and Greg. "There was a car crash near Florence," he said.

"One of the vehicles in the crash was a grey van. The men from the van ran away, but the police found your backpacks and other things stolen from tourists in the back of the van.

"I'm sorry to say they found no money, but the police will bring your backpacks here. So you have not lost everything."

The next morning, they got into Signore Berti's little truck. Many people from the village came to say goodbye.

"I'm sad we lost our money," said Greg. "But it has been a wonderful honeymoon, and we can come back."

"Of course," said Laura. "We must come back."

THANK YOU

Thank you for reading Travellers' Tales. (Word count: 6,411) We hope you enjoyed the stories.

If you would like to read more graded readers, please visit our website http://www.italkyoutalk.com

Other Level 3 graded readers include
A Dangerous Weekend
A Holiday to Remember
Akiko and Amy Part 1
Akiko and Amy Part 2
Akiko and Amy Part 3
Be My Valentine
Different Seas
Enjoy Your Business Trip
Enjoy Your Homestay
I'm Late!
I Need a Friend
Let's Do It!
Lincoln Takes a Trip
Match Day
Old Jack's Ghost Stories from England (1)
Old Jack's Ghost Stories from England (2)
Old Jack's Ghost Stories from Ireland
Old Jack's Ghost Stories from Japan

Old Jack's Ghost Stories from Scotland
Old Jack's Ghost Stories from Wales
Party Time!
Pretty and Bright
Roger's Long Ride
Rona
Stories for Christmas
The Curse
The Diary
Time to Go
Together Again
Who is Holly?
Wintertime

ABOUT THE AUTHOR

I Talk You Talk Press is an award-winning Japan-based publisher of language textbooks, graded readers and language learning/teaching resources. We won the Language Learner Literature Award in 2019 and 2020.

Our team is made up of highly experienced language teachers and translators, who have all studied at least one additional language to an advanced level.

This experience enables us to design our materials from the perspective of both the teacher and the learner. We consult with both teachers and language learners when designing our textbooks and graded readers, and test our materials extensively in the classroom before publication.

We are a fast-growing press, and currently publish graded readers for learners of English. We publish new graded readers monthly.